COUNTRY PROFILES

MALAYSIA

BY ALICIA Z. KLEPEIS

Blastoff! Discovery launches a new mission: reading to learn. Filled with facts and features, each book offers you an exciting new world to explore!

BLASTOFF! UNIVERSE

BLASTOFF! DISCOVERY

BLASTOFF! Beginners

BLASTOFF! READERS

GRADE K

GRADES 1-3

GRADE 4

This edition first published in 2022 by Bellwether Media, Inc.

No part of this publication may be reproduced in whole or in part without written permission of the publisher.
For information regarding permission, write to Bellwether Media, Inc., Attention: Permissions Department,
6012 Blue Circle Drive, Minnetonka, MN 55343.

Library of Congress Cataloging-in-Publication Data

Names: Klepeis, Alicia, 1971- author.
Title: Malaysia / by Alicia Z. Klepeis.
Description: Minneapolis, MN : Bellwether Media, Inc., 2022. |
    Series: Blastoff! discovery: country profiles | Includes index. |
    Audience: Ages 7-13 | Audience: Grades 3-6 | Summary:
    "Engaging images accompany information about Malaysia.
    The combination of high-interest subject matter and narrative text is
    intended for students in grades 3 through 8"– Provided by publisher.
Identifiers: LCCN 2021051750 (print) | LCCN 2021051751 (ebook)
    | ISBN 9781644876121 (library binding) | ISBN 9781648346231
    (ebook)
Subjects: LCSH: Malaysia–Juvenile literature.
Classification: LCC DS592 .K58 2022 (print) | LCC DS592 (ebook)
    | DDC 959.5–dc23/eng/20211022
LC record available at https://lccn.loc.gov/2021051750
LC ebook record available at https://lccn.loc.gov/2021051751

Editor: Kieran Downs   Designer: Brittany McIntosh

Printed in the United States of America, North Mankato, MN.

TABLE OF CONTENTS

TAMAN NEGARA NATIONAL PARK

CANOPY WALK

Mosquitoes buzz and birds call on a steamy morning in Taman Negara National Park. A group of schoolchildren is ready to explore the Canopy Walk through the **rain forest**. A sea of green leaves surrounds them. They spy wild pigs from their place high above the forest floor. Suddenly, a colorful five-bar swallowtail butterfly flies just above.

DANUM VALLEY

PANGKOR ISLAND

PETRONAS TOWERS

ZAHIR MOSQUE

In the afternoon, the students cruise along the Tahan River. A monkey hoots as it jumps from branch to branch. The group stops to swim in the cool water. A rushing waterfall greets them at the end of their journey. Welcome to Malaysia!

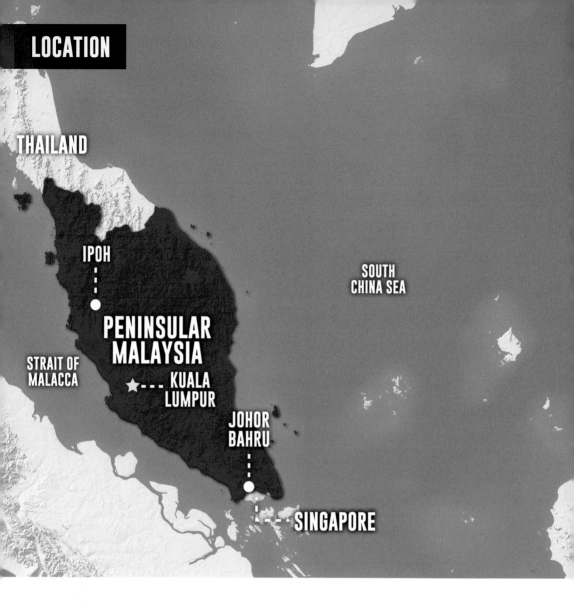

THAILAND

IPOH

SOUTH
CHINA SEA

PENINSULAR
MALAYSIA

STRAIT OF
MALACCA

KUALA
LUMPUR

JOHOR
BAHRU

SINGAPORE

Malaysia is a country in Southeast Asia. Its two separate
parts cover an area of 127,355 square miles (329,847 square
kilometers). **Peninsular** Malaysia is in the west on the Malay
Peninsula. Kuala Lumpur, the country's capital, is in western
Peninsular Malaysia. Thailand borders Malaysia to the north.
Drivers can reach Malaysia's southern neighbor, Singapore,
by bridge. The **Strait** of Malacca lies to the south and west.

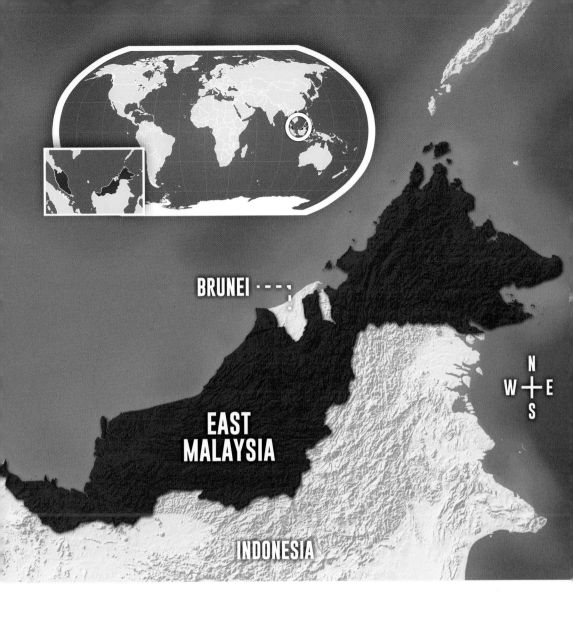

East Malaysia is about 400 miles (644 kilometers) away, across the South China Sea. It sits on the island of Borneo. Indonesia shares this island to the south. East Malaysia surrounds Brunei in the north.

Much of Peninsular Malaysia is mountainous and blanketed by rain forests. The Main Range runs down the middle. The Pahang River flows from the center of the peninsula.

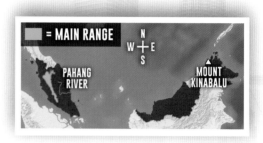

Coastal lowlands border the mountains on both sides of the peninsula. Beaches make up part of East Malaysia's coastal **plain**. Rain forests cover the land as it rises to hills and then mountains along the Indonesian border.

A MIGHTY MOUNTAIN

Malaysia's tallest mountain is Mount Kinabalu. It stands 13,435 feet (4,095 meters) high. Its peak has spiritual meaning to the Kadazan Dusun people.

Malaysia has a **tropical** climate. It is hot and **humid** throughout the country. Winds whip and heavy rains fall during **monsoon** seasons. Monsoons come from the southwest between June and September. They come from the northeast between November and March.

In the rain forests of Peninsular Malaysia, wild pigs root around in search of food to eat. Lesser mouse deer also scan the forest floor for leaves, shoots, and fruit. Clouded leopards prowl at night as flying foxes zoom through the trees.

Sun bears use their long tongues to find insects inside tree trunks. Tigers hunt for prey hidden in the forests. Pit vipers and green crested lizards sneak up on prey amidst the dense greenery. Bornean orangutans move easily through the trees of East Malaysia. They rest in nests that they make from plants.

FLYING FOX

BORNEAN ORANGUTANS

HELMETED HORNBILL

LAND OF THE HORNBILLS

The Malaysian state Sarawak is known as the Land of the Hornbills. The helmeted hornbill and the rhinoceros hornbill are two of the eight species found there.

SUN BEAR

CLOUDED
LEOPARD

CLOUDED
LEOPARD

Life Span: up to 15 years
Red List Status: vulnerable

clouded leopard range =

LEAST CONCERN	NEAR THREATENED	VULNERABLE	ENDANGERED	CRITICALLY ENDANGERED	EXTINCT IN THE WILD	EXTINCT

Over 33 million people live in Malaysia. More than two out of three are considered *bumiputra*. This group includes Malays and **native** peoples such as the Orang Asli and Dayak. About one out of five Malaysians is Chinese. Indians are another large group. Peninsular Malaysia is home to most of the nation's population.

Many people in Malaysia are Muslim. Islam is the official religion of Malaysia. Buddhists and Christians are also large religious groups. Most Malaysians speak Bahasa Malaysia. It is the nation's official language. English, Tamil, and Chinese are other common languages.

FAMOUS FACE

Name: **Henry Golding**
Birthday: **February 5, 1987**
Hometown: **Betong, Malaysia**
Famous for: **Actor who starred in films including *Crazy Rich Asians* and *Last Christmas***

SPEAK BAHASA MALAYSIA

ENGLISH	BAHASA MALAYSIA	HOW TO SAY IT
hello	apa khabar	AH-pah KAH-bahr
goodbye	selamat tinggal	seh-LAH-maht teen-GAHL
please	tolong	TAH-long
thank you	terima kasih	teh-REE-mah KAH-see
yes	ya	yah
no	tidak	TEE-dahk

KUALA LUMPUR

MAGNIFICENT MELAKA

Traders from around the globe helped build Melaka. Dutch traders constructed its red Christ Church. The Cheng Hoon Teng Temple is Chinese. The city became a UNESCO World Heritage site in 2008.

More than three out of four Malaysians live in **urban** areas. Kuala Lumpur is Malaysia's largest city. Over 8 million people call it home. Most people in cities live in apartments or townhouses. The wealthiest Malaysians may live in mansions. Most people travel by bus or car. Some take the train or ride a bicycle.

Houses in the Malaysian countryside are often built on stilts. They typically have metal or palm leaf roofs. Some people in **rural** East Malaysia live in longhouses. Several families can live together in these very large homes. Rural Malaysians often get around by motorcycle or even boat.

Music is a celebrated art form in Malaysia. Drums are important instruments. The single-headed *rebana* is featured in **traditional** music. The *geduk* is another common drum. It is made from a hollow tree trunk. Dance often accompanies the music. The *joget* is happy with quick movements. It is often performed at weddings and **cultural** events. Malaysian dancers often wear colorful costumes when performing traditional dances.

REBANA PERFORMANCE

BEAUTIFUL BATIK

Malaysians may wear traditional clothing made of *batik* fabric for formal occasions. Malaysian craftspeople use hot wax and colorful dyes to make this fabric.

Malaysian Muslim women commonly wear a knee-length shirt and long skirt with a head covering called a *tudung*. Muslim men typically wear black velvet caps during Friday prayer services. In cities, many Malaysians wear Western-style clothing.

Children in Malaysia start primary school at age 7.
They are required to attend for six years. Children in primary
school study math, science, Bahasa Malaysia, and English.
Students take an exam before they go on to secondary school.
General secondary school lasts for three years. After, students
may choose religious or **vocational** schools.

More than half of all Malaysians have **service jobs**. Many work in stores, transportation, or the government. Others have jobs in the **tourism** industry. Factories in Malaysia produce electronics, fabrics, and chemicals. Farms grow rice, coconuts, fruits, cocoa, and rubber.

PALM OIL

Malaysia is the world's second-biggest producer of palm oil.

19

SEPAK TAKRAW

Children and adults play soccer all across Malaysia. It is the nation's most popular sport. Many Malaysians enjoy badminton and rugby, too. *Sepak takraw*, also called kick volleyball, is a traditional Malaysian sport. Players must keep a ball in the air without using their hands. Flying kites is a popular activity in Malaysia. Near the coast, people often swim or relax on the beach.

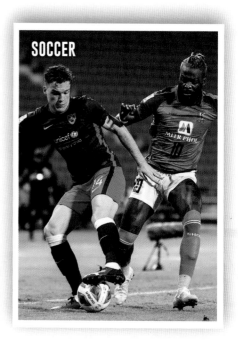

SOCCER

Young Malaysians often play video games. Shopping with friends is another common pastime. Families also go on road trips in their free time. Common destinations include cities, beaches, and parks such as Legoland.

LEGOLAND

MAIN GASING

Main gasing is a top-spinning game that is popular in Malaysia. Make your own spinning top. Have an adult help you make one!

What You Need:
- pencil
- cardboard
- scissors
- markers or crayons
- 4 pennies
- hot glue
- marble
- wooden chopstick or bamboo skewer

Instructions:
1. Trace a circle onto your cardboard and cut it out. Use your scissors to make a small hole in the center of this circle.

2. Draw designs or patterns on the top of the circle.

3. Glue four pennies onto the bottom (undecorated side) of the circle. Try to space them evenly apart and as close to the edge of the circle as possible.

4. Glue the marble over the hole on the same side of the circle as the pennies. Let it dry.

5. Flip over your circle so the pennies and marble are on the bottom. Place the chopstick or skewer into the hole and glue it. You might have to hold the chopstick in place until it dries. If your chopstick or skewer seems too long, you can have an adult help you use the scissors to cut it down.

6. Test out your top. How long can you make it spin?

INCREDIBLE ICE CREAM

Ice cream in Malaysia comes in many fantastic flavors. Dragon fruit and durian are two favorites. Chili chocolate, tea, and coconut rice are other cool choices.

RM 3.00

Many Malaysian meals are served with rice. Ginger, lemongrass, turmeric, and chili are commonly used spices. Malaysians often start their day with *nasi lemak*. People make it by cooking rice in coconut milk. They then add ingredients such as fried peanuts, fish, sliced cucumber, and a hard-boiled egg.

Fish or chicken curries are popular meals. *Satay* is grilled meat served on a stick. It is often served with peanut sauce. Chinese and Indian foods are common across Malaysia. Rose-flavored milk, nutmeg juice, and a special iced tea are just a few beverages Malaysians enjoy.

NASI LEMAK

SATAY

KUIH BAHULU

These spongy cakes are often eaten during special occasions. Have an adult help you make these cakes!

Ingredients:
3 eggs
1 cup sugar
1 teaspoon vanilla extract
1 1/4 cups flour
1/4 teaspoon baking soda
3 tablespoons canola oil or melted butter

Steps:
1. Preheat the oven to 375 degrees Fahrenheit (191 degrees Celsius).

2. Beat the eggs in a big bowl until fluffy and light. Add the sugar and keep beating until the sugar is dissolved. The mixture should be sticky.

3. Lightly oil a 12-cup muffin tin. Place in the preheated oven for two to three minutes and then remove from the oven and set aside.

4. Add the vanilla to the mixture. Fold in the flour, a little at a time. Mix in the canola oil or butter. Beat until blended well.

5. With a paper towel, have an adult carefully wipe out any oil in the muffin tin that looks dark. Fill each of the molds about three-quarters full.

6. Bake for roughly 15 minutes, until the cakes are golden in color.

7. Remove the cakes from the molds. Let them cool on a rack. Enjoy!

CELEBRATIONS

Many Malaysians celebrate Chinese New Year in January or February. Colorful dragon dances and huge family get-togethers mark the day. Ramadan is a month-long period of **fasting** for Muslims. Three days of feasting take place when Ramadan ends during *Hari Raya Aidilfitri*.

In May, Malaysian Buddhists celebrate Buddha's birth on Wesak Day. Followers may gather together to pray at temples. At night, decorated floats parade through the streets. August 31 is Independence Day. Malaysians mark their country's independence with parades, flying flags, and fabulous fireworks. Malaysians celebrate their culture and traditions all year long!

WESAK DAY

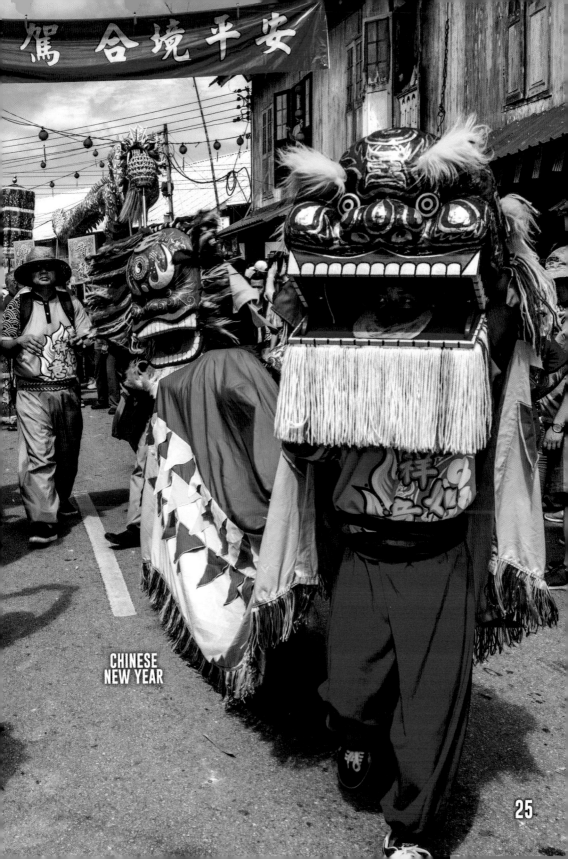

合境平安

駕

CHINESE
NEW YEAR

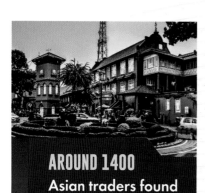

1826

Great Britain forms
the Straits Settlement,
a colony of Penang,
Melaka, and Singapore

AROUND 1400

Asian traders found
the port and trade
center of Melaka

1957

Malaysia gains its
independence from
Great Britain

AROUND 1400

Islam arrives
in Malaysia

1941

Japan invades Malaysia during
World War II and occupies the
country until 1945

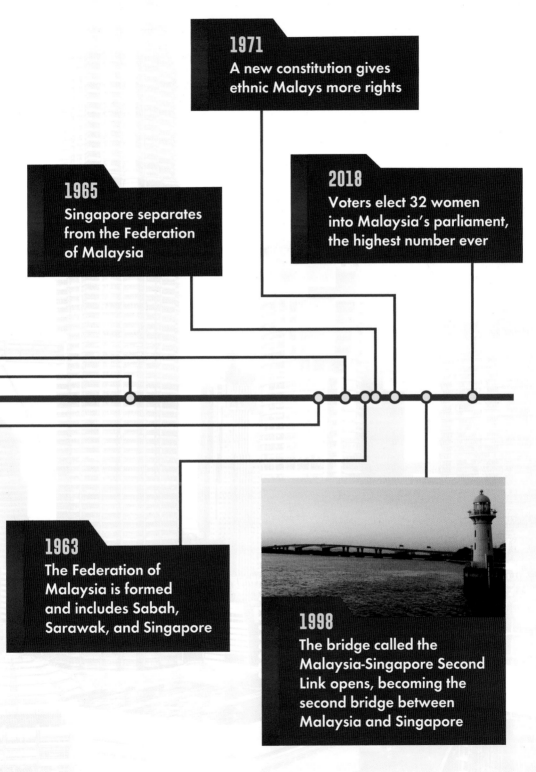

1971
A new constitution gives ethnic Malays more rights

1965
Singapore separates from the Federation of Malaysia

2018
Voters elect 32 women into Malaysia's parliament, the highest number ever

1963
The Federation of Malaysia is formed and includes Sabah, Sarawak, and Singapore

1998
The bridge called the Malaysia-Singapore Second Link opens, becoming the second bridge between Malaysia and Singapore

MALAYSIA FACTS

Official Name: Malaysia

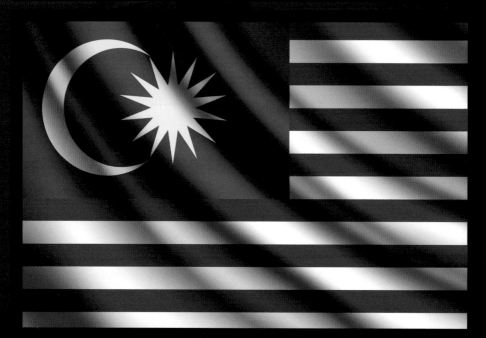

Flag of Malaysia: The flag of Malaysia has 14 alternating red and white horizontal stripes. These stripes represent the country's 13 states and the Malaysian federal territory. The red stands for bravery and the white for purity. In the flag's top left corner is a blue rectangle featuring a yellow crescent and a 14-pointed star. The crescent is a symbol of Islam. Yellow is the royal color of Malay rulers.

Area: 127,355 square miles
(329,847 square kilometers)

Capital City: Kuala Lumpur

Important Cities: Johor Bahru, Ipoh

Population:
33,519,406 (July 2021)

WHERE PEOPLE LIVE

COUNTRYSIDE
22.3%

CITY
77.7%

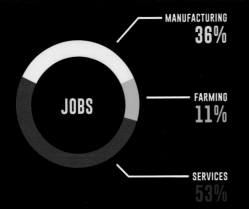

MANUFACTURING
36%

JOBS

FARMING
11%

SERVICES
53%

Main Exports:

electronics petroleum chemicals

natural gas palm oil rubber

National Holidays:
Independence Day (August 31),
Malaysia Day (September 16)

Main Language:
Bahasa Malaysia (official)

Form of Government:
federal parliamentary
constitutional monarchy

Title for Country Leaders:
prime minister (head of government), king (chief of state)

RELIGION

BUDDHIST
19.8%

OTHER
9.7%

CHRISTIAN
9.2%

MUSLIM
61.3%

Unit of Money:
ringgit

GLOSSARY

cultural—related to the beliefs, arts, and ways of life in a place or society

fasting—stopping the eating of all foods or particular foods for a time

humid—having a lot of moisture in the air

monsoon—related to winds that shift direction each season; monsoons bring heavy rain.

native—originally from the area or related to a group of people that began in the area

peninsular—relating to a section of land that extends out from a larger piece of land and is almost completely surrounded by water

plain—a large area of flat land

rain forest—a thick, green forest that receives a lot of rain

rural—related to the countryside

service jobs—jobs that perform tasks for people or businesses

strait—a narrow channel connecting two large bodies of water

tourism—the business of people traveling to visit other places

traditional—related to customs, ideas, or beliefs handed down from one generation to the next

tropical—part of the tropics; the tropics is a hot, rainy region near the equator.

urban—related to cities and city life

vocational—involved in the training of a skill or trade that prepares an individual for a career

TO LEARN MORE

AT THE LIBRARY

Joseph, Rahel, and Jo Kukathas. *Awesome Art Malaysia: 10 Works from the Land of Mountains Everyone Should Know.* Singapore: National Gallery Singapore, 2019.

Leaf, Christina. *Indonesia.* Minneapolis, Minn.: Bellwether Media, 2020.

Sullivan, Laura L. *Malaysia.* New York, N.Y.: Cavendish Square Publishing, 2019.

ON THE WEB

FACTSURFER

Factsurfer.com gives you a safe, fun way to find more information.

1. Go to www.factsurfer.com.

2. Enter "Malaysia" into the search box and click Q.

3. Select your book cover to see a list of related content.

INDEX

The images in this book are reproduced through the courtesy of: Patrick Foto, front cover; Ivsanmas, CIP, p. 28 (Malaysia flag); ThamKC/ Alamy Stock Photo, pp. 4-5; Nokuro, p. 5 (Danum Valley); shaifulzamri, p. 5 (Pangkor Island, Zahir Mosque); Igor Plotnikov, p. 5 (Petronas Towers); Alen thien, p. 8; Yusnizam Yusof, pp. 9, 22; OutdoorWorks, p. 9 (Kuala Lumpur); Anan Kaewhammul, p. 10 (sun bear); McPhoto/ Weber/ Alamy Stock Photo. p. 10 (flying fox); Sergey Uryadnikov, p. 10 (Bornean orangutan); ZakiFF, p. 10 (helmeted hornbill); glen gaffney, pp. 10-11 (clouded leopard); Sylvia sooyoN, pp. 12, 18; Featureflash Photo Agency, p. 13 (Henry Golding); Matyas Rehak, p. 13; SATHIANPONG PHOOKIT, p. 14; Christian Loader/ Alamy Stock Photo, p. 15; Mohd Shukri Mohd Yassin, p. 16; Ville Palonen / Alamy Stock Photo, p. 17; Genevieve Vallee/ Alamy Stock Photo, p. 19 (tour guide); Elizabeth Fitt/ Alamy Stock Photo, p. 19 (palm oil); Lano Lan, p. 20; mooinblack, p. 20 (soccer); abdrahimmahfar, p. 21 (Legoland); HariPrasetyo, p. 21 (main gaising top); Dan Kosmayer, p. 21 (main gaising bottom); Bored Photography, p. 23 (nasi lemak); dolphfyn, p. 23 (satay); Jeff Liou, p. 23 (kuih bahulu); Calvin Chan, p. 24; Chua Wee Boo/ Alamy Stock Photo, pp. 24-25; Derek Teo, p. 26; bemyself780, p. 27; NICK FIELDING/ Alamy Stock Photo, p. 29 (paper money); Vitoria Holdings LLC/ Alamy Stock Photo, p. 29 (coin).